Everybody Is Important

A Kids' Guide to Our Seven Principles

JENNIFER DANT

SKINNER HOUSE BOOKS
BOSTON

Printed in the United States

Principles page design by Kathryn Sky-Peck
Text page and cover design by Suzanne Morgan

ISBN 978-1-55896-564-5

6 5 4 3 2 1
13 12 11

Library of Congress Cataloging-in-Publication Data
Dant, Jennifer (Jennifer S.)
  Everybody is important : a kids' guide to our seven principles /
Jennifer Dant.
      p. cm.
  ISBN-13: 978-1-55896-564-5 (pbk. : alk. paper)
  ISBN-10: 1-55896-564-5 (pbk. : alk. paper)
 1. Unitarian Universalist Association—Doctrines—Juvenile literature.
I. Title.
  BX9841.3.D36 2011
  230'.9132—dc22
                        2010041587

The seven Principles of Unitarian Universalism

are promises that we make to each other and to ourselves that help us to be the best people we can be. The Principles are about how we should treat each other, what we love, and what we hope for ourselves and for all living things.

Every day gives us chances to put our Principles into action.

1

Every single person is important.

one

Today there's a stranger sitting next to Carla in math class. Carla's teacher, Mrs. Jackson, says the new girl's name is Patty. Mrs. Jackson asks the whole class to say "Welcome Patty!" together, but Patty just stares at her desk. Carla remembers her own first day at this school. It was so hard to find her way around, and everyone else seemed to know each other. When the bell rings for recess, everyone puts on their jackets to go to the playground. Mia, Carla's best friend, walks past the new girl and grabs Carla's arm. "Let's race to the swings!" she says.

 How do you think Patty feels about her first recess in a new school?

 What could Carla do next to make Patty feel welcome?

Jacob is standing in a long line of kids to buy apple juice in the school cafeteria. There's only one cash register open. The woman at the cash register is wearing a nametag that says "Rosie." Some of the kids are rolling their eyes and muttering about how slowly the line is moving. Rosie smiles at each kid and says "Have a good day" when she gives them their change, but most of them walk away without answering her or smiling back. When Jacob gets to the front of the line, Rosie sighs and rubs her eyes. "Have a good day," she says.

 Are the other kids treating Rosie like she's important?

 What could Jacob do differently than the other kids?

5

We treat

one another

with

respect.

two

Ginny's stomach aches terribly. She had a fight with her friend Lewis this afternoon, and now she doesn't want to eat dinner or talk to anybody. Ginny doesn't remember who got mad first, but she remembers that her face got hot and her voice got really loud. Remembering the mean and unfair things Lewis said makes her mad all over again. She thinks of what she wishes she'd said to him and writes it down in capital letters in her diary. But while she's writing, she starts to think of what she did say, and that makes her stomach hurt even more. She said things she didn't mean.

 How could Ginny show Lewis that she didn't mean what she said?

 What could Lewis do in return?

Inez, Tony, and Sandy are looking through Sandy's video games on a rainy Saturday afternoon. Tony sees a game he wants to play. Sandy tells Tony that her dad won't let her play that game until she's older. Inez makes a joke about playing "baby games" and Tony laughs. Sandy wishes that her friends would talk about something else or go home and leave her alone. She's not having fun anymore.

 Do you think Sandy's friends are treating her with respect?

 What could Sandy say to them about how she feels?

We spend our whole lives

learning how to be

the best people

we can be.

three

"**What** does that mean?" Lilly asks Maya about the necklace Maya's wearing, which has a little gold cup with a flame coming out of it. Maya explains that it's called a "flaming chalice" and is the symbol of her religion. "I'm a Unitarian Universalist," she tells Lilly. Lilly shows Maya her earrings, which are crosses hanging from little silver hoops. "My family believes that you have to get saved by Jesus to go to heaven." "We believe different things," Maya answers, "my family believes there are lots of ways to get to heaven." Lilly's eyes grow big. "But that's wrong!" she says.

 Do you think people can believe different things without fighting?

 What could Maya say back to Lilly?

Austin and his friend Carl are in Austin's backyard, waiting to go to the park. "It's not fair!" Austin yells at his mom, who is taking his baby sister out of her swing. "You said you would take us to the park!" His mom sighs. "I know we're late, Austin, but I still have to dress your sister and make you guys sandwiches before we can go." Austin groans. "But you promised we could go play basketball today and the other kids will be gone by the time we get there!" "I know and I'm sorry," Austin's mom says. Carl taps Austin on the shoulder while her back is turned. "Your mom has a lot to do. Maybe we could help her."

 Do you think Carl is helping Austin to be a better person?

 What could Carl and Austin do to help Austin's mom get ready to go to the park?

Together we learn about the world and what is true.

FOUR

Roger holds a hose over small plants poking through the ground. The sun is warm on his skin and reminds him of his grandmother saying that eating from a garden is like eating sunshine. Roger always thought it was a weird thing to say, but now it makes him smile. His grandmother loved working in her garden. After she died, the minister at her funeral said she was in heaven, but Roger's parents told him her body would go back to earth. Roger wonders where she really is now.

 Who could Roger talk to about his question?

 Do you think Roger will ever know for sure where his grandmother is now?

Joey is helping his mom set the table. "Cousin Bill is bringing his partner Tom over for dinner," Joey's mom says. Joey asks what "partner" means. "It means that Bill and Tom love each other and have decided to spend their lives together, like me and Daddy," she says. "Bill sounds really happy, and we're happy for him," she adds. Joey has known Bill his whole life and feels certain he wouldn't do anything wrong, but he has heard kids at school say mean things about men who live together.

Which do you think is more true—Joey's belief about Bill or what the other kids say?

What do you think Joey could say to the other kids about Bill and Tom?

Everyone
has the right
to use their
voice and be heard.

• • • •

five

Kristen has brought a backpack full of plastic animals to a sleepover. She dumps them out on the bed and calls out, "I get all the cats." "Hey, that's not fair," Dora answers, and Leah agrees. "But they're my animals," Kristen points out, "so I get to choose." Shrugging, Dora says, "I get the dogs then!" Leah slumps down and crosses her arms. She loves cats and dogs, and doesn't really feel like playing with the other animals. "What about me?" she thinks. "Doesn't anybody care which ones I want?"

 Do you think Leah should ask for what she wants?

 If she did, how do you think Dora and Kristen should respond?

Kamryn is showing the other kids how her hair is so long that she can braid it all by herself. She flips her braid over her shoulder and says, "Only girls with long hair are pretty." Marcus looks around at the other kids. "That's not true!" Marcus says. Gina is twisting one of her short dark curls around her finger and looking down.

 How do you think Gina feels about what Kamryn said?

 Do you think Marcus used his voice in a good way?

Together we work to

create a world that is

peaceful

and fair for everyone.

Andy's little brother Teddy loves singing. He sings in the shower, when he's walking to school, and sometimes even softly in bed before he goes to sleep. And when he sings in the school concerts, he has a big smile on his face. Andy's friends call Teddy a "sissy" and say it's "weird" that he would rather sing in the choir than play baseball or build forts after school. One day, Teddy cries and says, "Maybe I should just quit choir. Maybe then they'd stop teasing me!"

 Is it fair that Teddy is teased for liking to sing?

 Can you think of a way for Andy to help his little brother?

John has three dollars in his pocket. He's on his way to buy trading cards with it. As he walks, he keeps checking to make sure the money is still there. John earned the three dollars by helping his mom wash her car. He passes the church and remembers what the minister said last Sunday about the family whose house burned down on Spruce Street. The minister said that people could give money to help that family. John doesn't know the family, but he remembers seeing a picture of two kids standing in front of their ruined house.

 What do you think John should do with his three dollars?

 How do you think it would make the kids who lost their house feel to know that people want to help them?

We respect our earth and all living things.

seven

Anna and Riley have had a great day at the beach. They showed each other cool sea shells, made a sand castle, and stuck their feet in the cool clear water. "Time to go guys!" Anna's dad calls out. Anna and Riley begin picking up their beach toys and towels and chairs. Riley kicks over the castle. The soda can and old plastic fork they used for a tower and a flag pole are lying in the sand. "Grab that trash," says Anna. "Why?" asks Riley. "It was here when we got here."

 Why do you think Anna wants to pick up the trash?

 Does it matter that someone else left the trash in the first place?

Tyler has been spending the summer on his uncle Derek's farm. He has been helping his uncle to gather eggs from the chickens and feed the pig. His uncle takes very good care of the animals, feeding them food that they like and making sure they are healthy and comfortable. One day, Derek tells Tyler that he will eventually kill the pig for his family to eat. Tyler feels a little confused. "So why," he asks, "are you so nice to the pig now?"

 Why do you think Uncle Derek takes good care of the pig?

 Does it matter if a pig is healthy and comfortable?